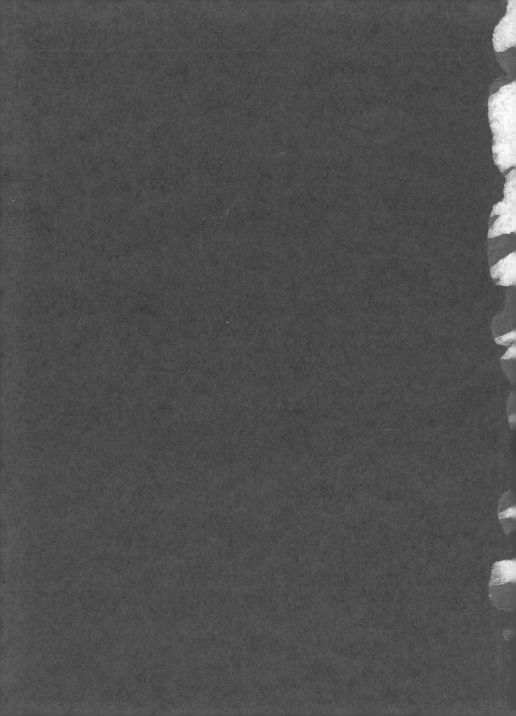

The
THANK YOU
Book

Hundreds of Clever,
Meaningful, and Purposeful
Ways to Say Thank You

ROBYN FREEDMAN SPIZMAN

LONGSTREET PRESS
Atlanta, Georgia

Published by
LONGSTREET PRESS
2140 Newmarket Parkway
Suite 122
Marietta, GA 30067

Second edition
1st printing 2001

This book is designed to provide general information in regard to the subject
matter covered. At the time of initial publication, all of the information is believed
to be accurate, however, some or all of the information is subject to change from
time to time and may no longer be free of charge or available. No warranties or
representations with respect to the information provided is made and neither the
publishers nor the author shall be liable for any loss or damage to persons or
property arising from the use of this book.

Printed in the United States of America

Library of Congress Catalog Card Number: 00-111985

ISBN 1-56352-651-4

Cover and book design by Jill Dible

Gratitude Is the Best Attitude

The Thank-You Book is presented to

_____

From

_____

"A friend is a gift you give yourself."

— ROBERT LOUIS
STEVENSON

Contents

"A day for toil,
an hour for sport,
But for a friend
is life too short."

— RALPH WALDO EMERSON

ACKNOWLEDGMENTS

⌇

I never miss an opportunity to say thank you, and here's my chance to do just that! My heartfelt thanks to my wonderful family and friends who fill my life with happiness and love. To my wonderful husband, Willy, and our two children, Justin and Ali, I am your biggest fans. My unending thanks for supporting my literary obsessions, for your support with everything I do, and for cheering me on. To my loving parents, Phyllis and Jack Freedman, who embrace the true meaning of "thank you" and define the word generous. To Doug and Genie Freedman, Sam Spizman, Gus Spizman, Lois and Jerry Blonder, Ramona Freedman, and Bettye Storne, who deserve a world of thanks. And to the late Regina Spizman and my beloved grandparents and family members who are greatly missed, I am thankful for your presence in my life.

I also wish to acknowledge my dear friend and one of my favorite authors, H. Jackson Brown, Jr., who wrote *Life's Little Instruction Book* and said, "Robyn, you can hit this one out of the ballpark." And to all the remarkable people at Longstreet Press, I am a fortunate person to have the guidance of such dedicated and hardworking souls.

And a special thanks to you, my readers, who will put these ideas to work and spread your kindness around the world, making it a better place in which to live. There is much work to be done and I am grateful to have you on board.

"It is more blessed to give than to receive."

— ACTS 20:35

INTRODUCTION

～～～

Over the years I've been blessed with a caring family and a circle of friends who have never missed an opportunity to do a good deed or share a kind word. A kiss, a hug, a sincere thank-you filled every get-together, and throughout my life at every turn, I have found that two simple little words have given me a great deal of satisfaction.

As a consumer advocate for the past twenty years in Atlanta, Georgia, and a gift-giving expert reporting nationwide, I have shown viewers how to express their thanks, appreciation, concern, and feelings to those they care about in creative and meaningful ways. This book is a collection of some of the ideas I have compiled over the years.

The saying "It's better to give than to receive" captures the true meaning of the words "thank you." When a thank-you is delivered with heartfelt feelings and put into words, it makes an indelible impression that is stored in one's memory bank forever. Giving thanks shouldn't be limited to Thanksgiving, a special holiday, or a particular occasion . . . it's a gift in itself.

When I reflect on the most meaningful gifts I have received, they are the handwritten thank-you notes and poems from my husband, our children Justin and Ali, and a dedicated circle of family and friends. From birthdays to anniversaries, "get well" occasions to no occasion at all, those little and big thank-yous have become lasting treasures.

As a little girl I always wrote my parents, teachers, family, and friends creative thank-yous and poems to express my appreciation. In fact, I'll always remember Mr. Cohen, the bicycle man, who framed my thank-you poem and proudly displayed it in his store. All it said was "Thank you Mr. Cohen, the world's best bicycle man . . . No one can fix a bike as good as you can!" I drew a picture of him fixing my bike and there was a big smile on the little girl's face. How small a deed, yet it was so greatly appreciated. My parents taught me at an early age that when life offers you a thank-you moment, you should grab it and express your heartfelt feelings.

Throughout our lives, we are given many types of gifts, yet some arrive without colorful wrapping paper or pretty ribbons. These thank-yous are gifts of the heart that tell us we've done a good job as a parent or made a difference in someone's life. One of those gifts arrived a few years ago when our daughter Ali, who is now fourteen, said she wanted to write a book. Ali attempted numerous ideas before finally deciding to write her own kid's version of *The Thank You Book*.

Ali's goal, like mine, was to inspire more thank-yous. Only her job was going to be much more difficult: she wanted to inspire other kids to say thank you *and* make it "cool" to do so. Both Ali and her older brother Justin were raised expressing their appreciation in writing, and I knew she had lots of creative ideas and understood the importance of gratitude. Ali spent months writing one chapter at a time, working long hours after all her homework was completed to compile her ideas. A computer wizard, she organized her chapters and announced she wanted to get it published. Talk about a gift! When we learned that my publisher, Longstreet Press, was excited about her book idea, we were thrilled. *The Thank You Book for Kids* by Ali

Lauren Spizman is indeed a gift for every child, and offers how-to advice for kids to help them write really fun and memorable thank-yous. I feel extremely fortunate to have Ali's wonderful help now in spreading my thank-you mission.

Living a life filled with a generous spirit offers endless rewards. Find someone in your life who deserves a thank-you, needs a hug or a kind word, and discover the real meaning of giving thanks. It's a lifelong love affair with caring, kindness, and the ability to truly appreciate others and let them know. In return, you'll discover more of life's little treasures. There is much work to do in this world when it comes to spreading kindness. Keep in mind that a thank-you is a gift and a boomerang in disguise. Once you give a thank-you, it has the incredible power to come right back.

*"The purpose
of life is a life
of purpose."*

— ROBERT BYRNE

Forever with Thanks

THANK YOU begins as two words we learn as children in response to the question, "What do you say?" Thank you starts out as an expected reply and often a household rule. However, the immeasurable joy in thanking someone comes once the real value of the action is understood, and long after you have received enough thank-yous in your life to know the real satisfaction of its action.

■ ■ ■

THANK YOU is the ultimate expression of appreciation that acknowledges someone's kindness and thoughtfulness. When saying "Thank you," you have an opportunity to let family or friends know how much their deed, words, or kindness meant to you. This immediate reciprocation validates and acknowledges the goodness that life has to offer and makes the good times better and the difficult times easier to swallow.

■ ■ ■

THANK YOU is about all the little details in life and our ability to accept the gifts of love and caring, no matter how big or how small. Accepting others' affection, love, or friendship and letting them know how much it means to you is an art. Thank you ultimately becomes the fine art of returning the expression of kindness, and fully participating in the true meaning of thoughtfulness and appreciation.

■ ■ ■

THANK YOU, when thoughtfully planned, is both a joy and a meaningful experience. How you choose to thank someone becomes a wonderful journey to express your uniqueness and in turn to celebrate another person's special qualities. Thank you is your opportunity to leave your mark in time, be creative, and show that you care about someone else while leaving your lasting imprint on another's memory.

■ ■ ■

THANK YOU is a two-way street. As you travel down the road of thanks, you will make more friends and discover the road to happiness. All of this plus the inner satisfaction that comes from taking the time to tell someone else he or she is special.

■ ■ ■

THANK YOU is not an end but a beginning. It's a lifelong celebration which allows you to take action and make the ordinary extraordinary!

Increase Your Thank-You Opportunities

Whom Are You Going to Thank?

Consider all of the people who are important to you in your life, and make a list of them. For just a moment, think of those on your list who mean the most. Think, too, of all those people who contribute daily to your life or the lives of those you care about. Now ask yourself, when was the last time I went out of my way to thank them? Not just for a gift or something they did for me, but a thank-you simply for loving me or caring about me? A thank-you for being my friend. A thank-you for being a thoughtful child, a helpful spouse, or the most wonderful relative?

Your life is filled with people to thank. Consider beginning each day with a thank-you motto: THANK FOUR PEOPLE EVERY DAY FOR SOMETHING! Get in the practice of saying thank you. Living a life of thanks takes time and effort, but the payoff is great! Thank the mailman for getting the mail to you every day, thank your dry cleaners for your clean clothing, thank a volunteer for her heart of gold, thank yourself for thanking others!

Look for ways to thank people, and you'll be surprised at the return. Thanking people is easy, and doesn't require any additional energy. It's one of life's little details that makes each day a little more meaningful and a lot more fun.

The thank-you spirit is a year-round opportunity, so challenge yourself to keep the promise and spread your thanks. Thank you is a sincere response to show how you feel. It's not a bribe or a way to win friends; it's a way to share yourself and your feelings with another person who deserves it.

Count how many people you thank today, and if you are not meeting your motto of THANK YOU FOR . . . four times a day, then regroup and try to increase your thank-yous daily. See how many people you can thank for something. Here are a few ideas to get you started:

- Thank you for listening.
- Thank you for following directions.
- Thank you for helping me.
- Thank you for making such a difference in my life.
- Thank you for such great service.
- Thank you for being so thoughtful.
- Thank you for being you.
- Thank you for such a good idea.
- Thank you for returning my call.
- Thank you for thinking of me.
- Thank you for loving me.
- Thank you for remembering me.
- Thank you for cleaning up.
- Thank you for being so neat.

- Thank you for being mine.
- Thank you for your great advice.
- Thank you for your words of wisdom.
- Thank you for understanding my feelings.
- Thank you for your encouragement.
- Thank you for being there for me.
- Thank you for appreciating me.

By saying thank you often, you will develop a habit of gratitude; it will enhance your own life as well as the recipients of your kind words.

CREATE A THANK-YOU PROJECT

Think of all the times you say thank you daily. Add a special touch to your thank-yous by starting a THANK-YOU PROJECT. You can spread your words of thanks and make them more memorable with either a business-style card or certificate that you make up in quantity and distribute daily to anyone you wish to thank. All you have to do is give someone a thank-you card, note, or personalized certificate that lets him know he is appreciated and deserves a thank-you.

Suggestions for Thank-You Cards

Please give this card to your employee: You are doing an excellent job and should be commended for your commitment to excellence! Keep up the great work!

Thank you for being so special. You are someone who makes a difference and deserves a thank-you.

I am spreading thank-yous to people who deserve them. You are someone special and I can see that you care about your job and helping others. Thank you for being you.

The Top Ten Thank-You Occasions

Graduations, weddings, and births are among the occasions of celebration and gift-giving that always call for a thank-you. Make it a regular practice to extend a formal thank-you when others acknowledge you in these special ways:

JUST MARRIED!

JUST GRADUATED!

JUST DID IT!

SYMPATHY WISHES

JUST FRIENDS

HAPPY BIRTHDAY!

GET WELL

IT'S A BABY!

HERE'S A GIFT

HAPPY ANNIVERSARY

"A day for toil, an hour for sport,
But for a friend is life too short."

— RALPH WALDO EMERSON

The Thank-You E-mail

With the help of the Internet, there are now hundreds of new ways to express your thanks in no time flat. I'm often asked if e-mail is an appropriate way to express your thanks. While I absolutely love e-mail, it is not always an appropriate substitute for a handwritten thank-you note, especially when you have been given a gift, or someone has really gone out of their way or done an extraordinary act of kindness. Some rules remain steadfast. Wedding gift thank-yous should always be written by hand, yet at other times it's acceptable to send an ASAP thanks in cyberspace. Whenever possible, I also like to call someone and thank them personally. This lets them know their gift arrived safely and is appreciated.

To every rule there are exceptions, and when you want to send an instant thank-you, e-mail can be a trusty resource. For the most part, though, "snail mail," as the cyberworld tags it, is still the time-honored and appropriate way to express thanks. With some flexibility in mind, save your e-mail thank-yous for thank-yous when time is of the essence.

E-mail, when put to use creatively and with thought, can be effective. The secret is to make your words jump off the screen, sending a great big hug in that person's direction. As they scroll down their messages, yours should stand out. For example, your message could read "A CYBER THANK-YOU TO THE

The Thank-You Chain Letter

Another way to participate in a THANK-YOU PROJECT is by starting
a thank-you chain letter award—much like the chain letters we
loved as kids. Consider writing a letter and sending it to one
friend whom you wish to thank. Ask the friend to then send it
to another friend and continue the chain without breaking it.
The letter front and back will be filled with names and will
"thankfully" continue all around the world.

Here is a sample letter you can use:

The Thank-You Award

You are receiving this THANK-YOU CHAIN LETTER because you are
a person who has shown immeasurable kindness and unending thoughtfulness. You deserve to be thanked for making
such a difference in my life as well as others. You have made
your corner of the earth more hospitable, gentler, and more
meaningful with your smile, good deeds, and wonderful ways.

Perhaps there is someone else you think deserves this THANK-
YOU CHAIN LETTER. Please sign your name and then send or give
this letter to whomever you think deserves it. If everyone thanks
one additional person for making his or her world a better place,
we all just might inspire more kindness and good deeds.

You are someone I am thankful for!

Sincerely,

(sign your name)

WORLD'S BEST FRIEND." Or, "A WORLD WIDE WEB OF
THANKS FOR YOU!" Simply, consider your e-mail as a thank-
you surprise and add some pizzazz. A little thought can often
go a long way on the Internet.

Here's a suggestion of one thank-you poem I sent when I was
under the weather and found myself short on time.

E-mail Thank You

Here's a cyber thank-you,
Since I couldn't wait to say . . .
You fill my life with happiness
Each and every day.

Your thoughtful deed was noticed,
You've been a friend right from the start.
This thank-you was sent in cyberspace,
But it came straight from my heart.

With cyber hugs, Robyn

"Most people are about as happy as they make up their minds to be."

— ABRAHAM LINCOLN

Thank-You Dos and Don'ts

HERE ARE SOME HELPFUL IDEAS WHEN SAYING THANKS:

Make the thank-you match the gesture. Be sure not to overdo or underplay a thank-you. Sometimes simply saying "thank you" is all that is necessary, while other times you need to do a little something extra.

Remember, a thank-you is always appropriate. No matter how big or how small an action, a thank-you is always the nice thing to do, and well deserved. Be sure to appreciate the little things in life and always say thank you.

Be timely with your thank-you. The sooner the thank-you, the better. If you are thanking someone verbally, do it as soon after the gesture as possible. If you are writing a note and have only a few to write, try to send it no longer than a week later. In the case of multiple gifts that require a thank-you, try and write the note four to six weeks later or as soon as possible. When it will take a while to write the note, confirm the thank-you verbally and follow it in writing.

Be specific with your thanks. When someone does something nice for you or shows her appreciation in some way, be sure to thank her by specifically commenting on her deed. "I really appreciated your thoughtfulness when you sent me that greeting card in the mail. You must have really searched hard for such a perfect card. I'm saving it for a rainy day to cheer me up."

Add your personal touch. Creativity comes in all shapes and sizes and suits all budgets. You don't have to spend a lot of money to be creative. Your thank-you, however, will have far greater meaning if you take the time to add a personal touch.

Plan ahead. There are certain times of the year when thank-yous are predictable. From holidays to the end of the school year, think ahead and enjoy taking your time with the creation of each expression of thanks.

Involve others when possible. Set an example and involve the kids or your entire family and make "thank-yous" together. Teach kids early on to write thank-you notes, and always have a thank-you rule . . . you get to play with the toy once you call Aunt Francie and say thank you!

Use the "thank-you motto" and be prepared! Have a selection of greeting cards, including blank ones, on hand for those "pop up" thank-yous. Sometimes you don't have time to run out and be thoughtful, so put away a few items that are ready and waiting at your fingertips.

Save your favorite thank-yous and record them in this book.
Once in a while a special saying or a beautiful passage comes
your way that you know will brighten someone else's day.
Record it in the back of this book, and create a thank-you
legacy for generations to come.

*"Always be
a little kinder
than necessary."*

— JAMES M. BARRIE

Well-Matched Thank-Yous

The more you know about someone, the better suited your thank-you will be. Remember, it's the little things that count, like finding out someone's favorite color or favorite thing to eat. It's also fun to learn something new about the person, and he will appreciate your thank-you even more.

Use the following survey to match your thank-you with a few of his favorite things in life. Find out what he really likes, then select a thank-you that reflects it.

THANK-YOU WISH LIST

Favorite candy _____

Favorite color _____

Favorite food _____

Favorite snacks _____

Favorite hobbies _____

Favorite restaurant _____

Favorite things to do _____

Favorite music _____

Favorite song _____

Favorite singer _____

Favorite animal _____

Favorite perfume _____

Favorite saying _____

Favorite TV show _____

Favorite sport _____

Favorite thing to collect _____

Favorite book _____

Favorite childhood memory _____

Favorite hero _____

Favorite historical figure _____

Favorite celebrity _____

Favorite movie _____

Favorite childhood friends _____

Favorite thing to talk about _____

Favorite style of art _____

Favorite flower _____

Thank-You Gems and Birthstones

Personalize your thank-you by focusing on the day or month the person was born. Highlight how special that day was, and find out information that will help personalize your thank-you. Information about someone's horoscope or astrological sign often can be helpful and interesting in a thank-you.

Gems and birthstones are also a personal way to show your thoughtfulness, with words of praise or thanks that reflect the person's birth month.

CLEVER PHRASES

"My warmest thanks to a real jewel."

"How do I thank someone as precious as you?"

"Thank you to one of my most treasured friends."

"You're a jewel of a friend."

"No one can outshine you."

"You're someone I really value."

BIRTHSTONES

January GARNET	*July* RUBY
February AMETHYST	*August* PERIDOT, SARDONYX
March AQUAMARINE, BLOODSTONE	*September* SAPPHIRE
April DIAMOND	*October* OPAL, TOURMALINE
May EMERALD	*November* TOPAZ, CITRINE
June PEARL, MOONSTONE, ALEXANDRITE	*December* TURQUOISE, ZIRCON

What's in a Name?

Here's an idea for some light-hearted fun. Take a look at these examples of ways to use people's names to creatively say thank you. Refer to a dictionary if you need assistance. You'll enjoy the outcome of your efforts, and you're bound to make someone smile. They'll think you sat up all night thinking of this!

ACRONYMS

Use the alphabet letters to spell out an acronym of the person you are thanking:

Janie — Just About the Nicest Individual on Earth

Alf — Amusing Likeable Friend

Gail — Great Adult I Like!

Justin — Just Understanding, Super, Terrific, Irresistible & Nice

Ali — Always Likeable and Interesting

Tom — Terrific Outgoing Male

Patty — Pretty Amazing Terrific Thoughtful You

Billy — Brainy Intelligent Likeable Loveable You

Kevin — Kind Entertaining Vivacious Interesting and Nice

Susan — Super Unique Sweet And Number 1!

Susan — Sexy Unbelievable Sensational And Nice

Mom — Marvelous Overwhelmed and Mine!

Dad — Dedicated Amazing & Determined

Aunt — Always Utterly Noticeably Terrific

Uncle — Unbelievable Nice Clever Leading Example

Teacher — Terrific Educator Always Caring Happy Ecstatic Reasonable

THE NAME GAME

Think of clever ways to use a person's name, from rhyming the name to quoting a famous saying. The perfect thank-you shows thought, and what better way than to use the recipient's name. Your personal touch will always be remembered and everyone will think you're very witty. Here are some examples:

Great Scott!

Mary, Mary, You are very . . .

Action Jackson!

Mark my word, Thank you Mark

You left your Mark . . .

I hit the Jack-pot when I met you, Jack!

I Believe in Steven

Jerry, you are very . . .

Always ready is our Bettye

If anyone can, Anne can!

You were Just-in time!

Willy or won't he?

You're always Karen

Al, that's my pal!

Chuck brings us luck . . .

"One man with courage is a majority."

— ANDREW JACKSON

Everyday Thank-Yous

B e prepared to thank someone and have on hand a variety of simple and thoughtful items that will help accomplish your thanks. Don't procrastinate, and go out today and purchase ten or more greeting cards that say "Thank you," "I'm thinking of you," or any expression that you find touching and meaningful. You'll save both time and money if you stock up in advance, and you'll be prepared for thanking someone instantly. Store and organize the cards or items in a special box, closet or drawer and refill as needed. Below are necessary items to include:

THE THANK-YOU SURVIVAL KIT

- *The Thank-You Book*
- greeting cards for all occasions
- blank notes
- sympathy notes
- small, generic gift books
- a box of candy
- personalized stationery
- a few children's toys
- sweets and treats
- chicken soup in the freezer
- self-sticking notes—for when you're in a hurry
- a favorite book
- gift bags
- gift-wrapping paper
- tape
- scissors
- ribbon
- stickers
- stamps

"That it will never come again, Is what makes life so sweet."

— EMILY DICKINSON

The Thank-You Thesaurus

If you're at a loss for words or find yourself using the same adjectives frequently, consider ways that you can vary your sentiments of gratitude. Never get into the rut of always saying the same thing when you express yourself. The following words will be useful when expressing your feelings of thanks:

WORDS TO DESCRIBE YOUR FEELINGS OF THANKS

delighted	touched
honored	moved
thankful	inspired
appreciative	speechless
grateful	complimented
obliged	enjoy
beholding to	relish
indebted to	ecstatic

WORDS TO DESCRIBE THE GIFT OR DEED YOU ARE THANKFUL FOR

captivating	genuine
irresistible	exquisite
charming	state-of-the-art
lovable	magical
adorable	ravishing
colorful	stylish
gracious	outrageous
exciting	phenomenal
fabulous	awesome
gorgeous	cuddly
memorable	picture-perfect
moving	whimsical
lovely	eye-catching
soothing	special
friendly	elegant
amazing	exceptional
striking	high-tech
sensational	outstanding
thoughtful	luxurious
dazzling	mouthwatering
stunning	delectable
unforgettable	unparalleled
remarkable	unique
superb	prize-winning
glorious	knockout
monumental	sumptuous
pleasurable	compelling

THANK-YOU WITH COMPLIMENTS

While flattery might get you anywhere, it must be truthful and sincere in order to be meaningful. Try some of these statements when you wish to thank someone with compliments! Flattery is the gift of making others feel good about themselves. The fact that you notice their special traits or a certain talent they have will be greatly appreciated.

Here are some complimentary statements to get you started:

"You are one of my favorite people to talk with.
You are so interesting."

"You are one of the smartest people I know!"

"Your excellent taste shows up in everything you do."

"Your bright ideas make everything you touch better."

"You always know the perfect thing to say and do."

"You will always be my mentor and someone I look up to."

"You are the world's best friend.
How could I ever get along without you?"

"You are not only my parent, but the wisest person I know."

"You have such insight."

Thank-You Note Statements That Compliment

"You have outdone yourself. Of course, you always do."

"Your outstanding taste is reflected in your beautiful gift."

"I will always treasure your gift and most of all the beautiful
thoughts that accompanied it."

"A special person like you deserves the best."

"This gift was definitely a tribute to your excellent taste."

"Your beautiful gift is only matched by your continued caring."

"Leave it to creative you to find such a fabulous gift."

"You both are the perfect pair and represent a
role model for us to follow."

"I could never fill your footsteps, but will be inspired by your
gesture and beautiful book of wisdom."

"Every time I look at your gift, I will think of
your unending thoughtfulness."

"You are one in a million, and I'm so lucky to
call you my friend."

"My thanks to you for being someone I can
count on no matter what."

ACCEPTING A COMPLIMENT

The art of accepting a compliment goes hand in hand with the art of saying thank you. Accepting a compliment is a special opportunity to show your appreciation in a different way to someone who took the time to praise you. Compliments are meant to make you feel good, and what better way to return the favor than to accept the compliment gracefully by letting someone know how much you appreciate his or her kind words?

Many people have trouble accepting a compliment. They brush them off, are embarrassed, deny their possibility, or simply refuse to accept them. A compliment, like a thank-you, is a gift. It's a moment when someone cares enough to share their positive feelings with you. In return, a thank-you is most appropriate. You can be humble and honored at the same time, so the next time someone gives you a compliment, look the giver right in the eye and say "Thank you!" with a smile. You'll feel good about it and so will they.

Just say thank you!

"Happiness makes up in height for what it lacks in length."

— ROBERT FROST

Famous Thank-You Quotations

⌒⌒⌒

Fine poetry—the distilled, lyrical language of poets and writers throughout the ages—lends itself beautifully to thank-yous. When you are at a loss for words, try quoting these famous thank-yous:

"Well done is better than well said."
— BEN FRANKLIN

"Treasure the love you receive above all. It will survive long after your gold and good health have vanished."
— OG MANDINO

"The purpose of life is a life of purpose."
— ROBERT BYRNE

"It is one of the most beautiful compensations of life that no man can sincerely try to help another without helping himself."
— RALPH WALDO EMERSON

"A day for toil, an hour for sport,
But for a friend is life too short."
— RALPH WALDO EMERSON

"A friend is a gift you give yourself."
— ROBERT LOUIS STEVENSON

"Most people are about as happy as they
make up their minds to be."
— ABRAHAM LINCOLN

"It is a wise father that knows his own child."
— SHAKESPEARE, *KING LEAR*, I, IV

"Some goals are so worthy, it's glorious even to fail."
— UNKNOWN

"Grow old along with me!
The best is yet to be,
The last of life, for which the first was made."
— ROBERT BROWNING, *RABBI BEN EZRA*

"To have a friend, be a friend."
— OLD SAYING

"I shall return."
— DOUGLAS MACARTHUR,
AFTER LEAVING THE PHILIPPINES, MARCH 1942

"It is more blessed to give than to receive."
— ACTS 20:35

"Nothing great was ever achieved
without enthusiasm."
— RALPH WALDO EMERSON, *CIRCLES*

"Nothing great in the world has been
accomplished without passion."
— HEGEL, *PHILOSOPHY OF HISTORY*

"It is by forgiving that one is forgiven."
— MOTHER TERESA,
FOR THE BROTHERHOOD OF MAN

"To err is human, to forgive, divine."
— ALEXANDER POPE, *AN ESSAY ON CRITICISM*

"A friend may well be reckoned the masterpiece of nature."
— RALPH WALDO EMERSON, *FRIENDSHIP*

"A friend is a person with whom I may
be sincere. Before him, I may think aloud."
— RALPH WALDO EMERSON

"A true friend is the most precious of all possessions and
the one we take the least thought about acquiring."
— LA ROCHEFOUCAULD, *MAXIMS*

"Think big thoughts, but relish small pleasures."
— H. JACKSON BROWN, JR.

"A joy that's shared is a joy made double."
— ANONYMOUS,
RECORDED BY JOHN RAY, *ENGLISH PROVERBS*

"That it will never come again,
Is what makes life so sweet."
— EMILY DICKINSON

"The heart that loves is always young."
— ANONYMOUS (GREEK PROVERB)

"Happiness is an inside job."
— H. JACKSON BROWN, JR.

"Always be a little kinder than necessary."
— JAMES M. BARRIE

"One man with courage is a majority."
— ANDREW JACKSON

"Whoever is happy will make others happy too.
He who has courage and faith will never perish in misery."
— ANNE FRANK

"A kind heart is a fountain of gladness, making everything in its vicinity freshen into smiles.
— WASHINGTON IRVING

"Happiness makes up in height
for what it lacks in length."
— ROBERT FROST

"One can never pay in gratitude; one can only
pay 'in kind' somewhere else in life."
— ANNE MORROW LINDBERGH

"The most exquisite pleasure is giving pleasure to others."
— JEAN DE LA BRUYÈRE

"There is as much greatness of mind in
acknowledging a good turn as in doing it."
— SENECA

"A friend is a person with whom I may be sincere. Before him, I may think aloud."

— RALPH WALDO EMERSON

Multiple Thank-Yous

Sometimes there are hundreds of people who need to be thanked, and this can be quite an ordeal if you are not organized. Here are some tips to help you when you are bombarded with thank-yous:

GET ORGANIZED

- An address system is absolutely necessary for thank-you notes, reply cards, sympathy acknowledgments, or any response you must make to multiple kind gestures. Some helpful ideas include:

- Keep a filing-card system with every address in alphabetical order of those you correspond with. Separate the files into categories like friends, family, business acquaintances.

- Address your thank-you notes ahead of time to correspond with your guest list. You might waste a few, but generally you'll save time and be able to focus better on the thank-you note.

- Write a few a day. Set a number—say, four—that must be done each day and stick to it. Before you know it, they'll all be done, and each day you'll feel good about your efforts.

• Avoid writing the same handwritten note to common groups of friends. Everyone wants to be acknowledged with your personal touch, and thank-you cards that are generic and mass produced often look that way and lack sincerity.

• Enlist the help of friends. Your friends or family will be delighted to help you write notes in a difficult time or time of need. Have a thank-you party and let each person write a dozen notes on your behalf and sign your name. Or, you could dictate what you want to say and they could be recorded.

• If you work on a computer, investigate special-event organizational programs (available at most computer stores) that help you organize all of your addresses, guests lists, etc.

■ ■ ■

MANY THANKS
Preprinted Notes

A personalized note is always appropriate when possible, but in situations like death or illness a preprinted acknowledgment card is certainly all that is needed. Some people find it therapeutic to write their own messages inside each card, but the acknowledgment itself is definitely acceptable.

When time is a factor, someone in the family is ill, or you must reach masses and cannot write a personalized note, here are some clever ideas that will help:

Write a humorous poem and have duplicates printed:

Humpty Dumpty sat on a wall
And look who joined him and had a great fall.
All the king's horses,
And all the king's men,
Are still working on putting
me back together again!

I'll be well soon and can't wait to thank you in person.
Your generosity is appreciated!

Sincerely,
Alan (a.k.a. Humpty)

■ ■ ■

You deserve a break today . . .
I've already had one!
I'll be back on my feet soon.

See you then,
Jerry

ADVERTISE YOUR THANK-YOU

If there is a newspaper or newsletter that is distributed to a majority of your friends who thought of you, a published note is a clever method of thanking them. Purchase or get extra copies and have a stack on hand. Here is a suggestion for your ad:

> **THANK-YOU SALE**: Closing out thank-you inventory and offering endless appreciation to caring friends and family members. Every thank-you must go. Making room for good health. First 100 people receive hugs.
>
> (your name)

■ ■ ■

Be Resourceful

Locate an item that comes in bulk and is inexpensive, but unique and out of the ordinary. For example, order 500 inexpensive business cards (as cheap as $16.00 for 500) and print up a clever message. Either send them out in an envelope or have a friend or colleague give them out at work for you.

> I'll be back to business as usual when I'm feeling better! This card guarantees you one gigantic thank-you when I see you in person.
>
> Sincerely,
>
> Bettye Storne

Thank You, My Friend

One of life's greatest gifts is friendship. Old friends, new friends, fast friends—they all have the ability to make a significant difference in your life. Thanks to friends, celebrations are sweeter and difficult times are easier to take.

There are many occasions and reasons for thanking friends. Real friends always seem to pop up during those trying moments, and they continue to spread sunshine wherever they go. Being a friend who is ready to help, care, or extend that special thank-you or meaningful gesture makes life so much richer. Thanking a friend is something very special, but keep in mind that friendship is like a diamond in the rough. How you care for the stone, encourage its uniqueness, and then enjoy its brilliance is what propels a friendship even further. There are no two diamonds in the world alike, or any two friendships. Care for each as though it is priceless.

When you thank a friend, you have a wonderful chance to really show your sensitivity to another's needs. It also feels wonderful to thank a friend. Here are some clever ideas for thanking yours:

World's Best Friend: Give your friend an award. Office or teacher supply stores sell awards of all shapes and sizes, or make your own from a piece of blue ribbon. Choose a first-place award for your friend and tell him he is #1 with you.

Carpool Coupon: If your friend feels like a taxi driver, give the gift of a carpool coupon and a day off! Cover a coupon book page with white paper and draw in your own coupon good for one day's driving.

Running Buddies: Thank your friend for being a running buddy with either a basket or bag of nylon stockings just her size. Find out the brand she prefers and then purchase a bunch of them. Or try filling a nylon knee-high stocking with hershey kisses and tie off the end for a clever "stocking stuffer" gift wrap.

Freezer Pleasers: Every friend loves a frozen meal good for a night when he doesn't want to cook. Purchase frozen specialty meals or snacks, or make your own. Your friend will really appreciate this one.

You Suit Me to a Tea! Fill up a coffee mug or a paper bag with tea bags or a sampling of gourmet teas, and arrive with your gift at tea time, accompanied with cookies and tea-time treats.

Get Organized: Give a clutter-free gift with a few hours of your time. If you've got the organizational know-how, use it to show a friend who needs help straightening up. Bring a few containers, file folders, and odds and ends and get rid of the clutter by grouping things together, setting up a file system, or cleaning up a drawer! Or, fill a basket or shopping bag full of organizational gadgets and your favorite organizers.

Friends' Night Out! Plan a special evening for you and your friend and have a friends' night out. Pick out a place for a light dinner and choose a movie neither of you have seen. Make your friends' night out a monthly or yearly get-together.

Good-deed Basket: Pack a basket of Band-Aids, chicken soup, bath soaps, or anything that would be comforting and attach this note and bring it to a friend: *A friend in need is a friend indeed! Need a friend? You can count on me!*

Support the Girl Scouts: Give a box of their famous chocolate thin mint cookies and attach a note . . . this gift was "meant" for you!

Songs of Friendship

Send a copy of the song "That's What Friends Are For" by Dionne Warwick, and include a note that says, *"When I hear this song I think of you!"*

Other Songs of Friendship

"Bridge Over Troubled Water" "You've Got a Friend"
Simon and Garfunkel   James Taylor

"Say 'Thank You'"
Craig N' Co.

FRIENDLY THANK-YOU NOTES

Use these thank-you notes and sayings for thanking your friends. If the thank-you note fits, then feel free to use it. However, for a thank-you note that will always be treasured, it's always best to add your special touch and personalize it in some additional way. Here are some ideas that might help you get started in writing a personalized thank-you note to a friend:

Thank-you Tips

Make references in your thank-you note to some of these points:

When was the first time you met?

What do you like most about your friend?

What was the most fun you ever had with your friend?

Recall a good deed that your friend did for you and mention it.

How has this friend impacted your life?

What do you admire about this friend?

FRIENDLY THANK-YOU POEMS

In good times and in bad times
My friend, you're always there.
And that is why I'm thankful
That about me you do care.

Friends like you don't
grow on trees
That's why I'm glad
that you picked me.

I'm always glad
that I am home,
When you call me
on the telephone.
So thank you for
your thoughtful ways
For brightening up all my days.
Thank you for the
love you show
For all the caring you bestow.

If I were to go shopping
for a brand new friend
I'd search the mall
from end to end.
I'd only want the very best
That's why I'd pick you
and leave the rest.

Thank you is
a simple word,
A common phrase
we all have heard.
But thank you now
means something new
Because, my friend,
I'm thanking you.

How can I thank my friend?
Let me count the ways,
I'll wear your gift
a thousand times
And thank you every day!

Friends may come
and friends may go,
But you're a friend
I'm glad I know.

Friends are rare
this thought is true,
That is why
I treasure you.

Friendly Thank-You Notes

Dear Lorie,

How do I ever begin to thank you for being such a wonderful friend? The best part of our relationship is that we both know how special we are to each other. Thank you for always cheering me up, and for never being too busy to listen. You always have something kind or comforting to say, and your advice has steered me in the right direction again and again.

I also want to thank you for sharing my hard times and my happy times. Your friendship and love help make each one of them better. When I met you, I made a friend for life. You will always remain close to my heart.

Forever your friend,

Janet

■ ■ ■

Dear Patty,

What in the world would I ever do without a friend like you? You always arrive to help me at the perfect time and seem to read my mind. It is such a comfort to me to know that no matter how often we speak or see each other, the second we are together it's as if we were never apart.

I am truly grateful for your friendship, and for your readiness to share anything and everything.

Love,

Susan

Dear Ava,

Friends like you are one in a million, and I can't begin to thank you enough for thinking of ways to add happiness to my life. You always know what I'm thinking, and it is so wonderful to know someone loves me just for being me. It's friends like you that make life so special.

What would I ever do without your brilliant opinion and insightful wisdom? Thank you, Alexander Graham Bell, for inventing the telephone, and thank you, Ava, for the times we shared on it!

Love,
Gail

■ ■ ■

Dear Julie,

Once upon a daydream, I heard a voice ask, "What's the nicest gift anyone can give?"—to which my immediate answer was "Love."

But the voice said, "Love is more what you are than what you give. Perhaps the greatest gift of all is friendship." And so I thought about that.

Thank you for being such a loving friend and for being mine. You have blessed me with life's greatest gift of all.

Always,
Bert

Dear Jim,

Whenever I think of the special people who have impacted my life with their wit, wisdom, and friendship, you immediately rise to the top. Your friendship and caring have served as a daily reminder that someone cares about me, and for that I am eternally grateful. Thank you for being that special friend, who makes time stand still and puts the fun back into my hectic life.

Gratefully,

Cheryl

■ ■ ■

Dear Marla,

How lucky I feel that somewhere along the way, I became your friend and you mine. I feel as if I have known you forever and am so fortunate to be blessed with such a caring and compassionate friend. How can I ever thank you enough for choosing me as your friend from the hundreds of people you meet daily? I knew when we first met that we were destined to become lifelong soul mates, and I remain eternally grateful to call you my friend.

Always,

Tracy

Dear Linda,

I'll always remember the happy times, the laughter and friendship that we have shared over the years. There's something very special about old friends, and boy, are we getting old! Friends like you continue to be a source of comfort that will remain with me for the rest of my life. Every time we are together I find myself feeling especially appreciative for the memories we have and thankful for the wonderful ones we continue to make.

Love always,
Wendy

■ ■ ■

Dear Betty,

Knowing you are my friend has given me added confidence in my life. You probably didn't know you had such magical powers, but your friendship and support have added a special ingredient to my life. No matter what occurs, I always know you are there with your bits of wisdom and your unending help. Thank you for being a friend I value.

Sincerely,
Beth

Dear Peter,

Through the years you have always stood by me as a loyal friend. And once again you arrived with your friendship and care for my well-being. Sometimes life poses difficult challenges, but with a friend like you I always know I have a place to turn when I need advice or help. Thank you for being that friend.

Sincerely,

Lyons

■ ■ ■

Dear Marianne,

What in the world would I do without your wonderful advice, sincere caring, and unconditional friendship? You have always given me time and understanding; whatever is on my mind is on yours, too. You have taught me so much about myself, and I'm lucky to have you as my teacher and friend. We have a very special friendship that I will always treasure, and I adore you for just being you.

Love,

Lisa

■ ■ ■

Dear Sarah,

When I thought it wasn't possible, you said I could do it! Your friendship and belief in me mean so much, and I will always be here for you. To try and thank you for being my friend would require a lifetime, but I hope you know how dear to my heart you will always be.

Thank you for being my friend!

Love,

Candy

Dear Carla,

Where do I begin to thank you for being my friend? You always know how to cheer me up. I could never begin to thank you enough for always being there for me. You are a beautiful and caring friend and my life is blessed because you are in it.

Love always,

Lorie

■ ■ ■

Dear Bob,

Friends like you have added so much to my life. Besides the fact that you keep such great company, you've got that charismatic ability to make everyone like you. I feel very fortunate that we became such good friends. You are someone I really look up to.

Your friend,

Sam

■ ■ ■

Dear Lori,

I just wanted to take a moment to share some special thoughts with you. When I saw you at the restaurant the other day, it struck me that you are one of those people in my life whom I label special for many reasons. Special is a word I use for people who have a dramatic impact on my life. You are that treasured friend who has forever changed my life.

Lots of love,

Janet

Dear Steve,

Although we seldom speak, when we do it brightens up my day. Your friendship has always served as a reminder of the good old days. I will never forget how you helped me during an important time in my life.

Your smile and wonderful sense of humor will always remain with me. Should you ever need me in any way, don't hesitate to call. Thank you for being my friend.

Love,
Susan

■ ■ ■

Dear Bettye,

How in the world could we ever get along without you as our friend? You have stood by us unconditionally and have been a great sense of strength in both good times and bad. When we think back to the day we met you, we know it was one of the luckiest days in our lives. Your laughter and kind ways have filled our home and our hearts; forever we will treasure your friendship.

The greatest definition of the word friend is you, Bettye.

We love you,
The Spizmans

■ ■ ■

Dear John,

You have always been such a special friend, and I remember liking you immediately the moment we met. You share my enthusiasm about life, and I absolutely love sharing my ideas with you. Thank you for taking such an interest in me and appreciating all the things I do. I will forever treasure your friendship.

Always,
Genie

■ ■ ■

Dear Larry,

No deed is too big or too small for our dear friend Larry. It seems as if whatever we need, you are there in a minute's notice. It was you who introduced us to the best ice cream parlor we've ever been to, and it continues to be you, Larry, who sweetens our life with your unending kindness and thoughtful ways.

A cherished friend comes along once in a million years, and you are truly one in a million.

Love always,
Willy

■ ■ ■

Dear Robyn,

"Friends are the family we choose for ourselves." These powerful words need no explanation. I want to thank you for making my birthday a very special day for me. The pearl earrings are just beautiful, and I have enjoyed wearing them several times. Lunch was delicious, and getting together with good friends is what makes life so much fun!

Again, thanks for being there for me. Your friendship is one that I'll always treasure.

Love,
Patty

Dear Meredith,

Thank you for believing in me and for saying the words that I really needed to hear. Your friendship means the world to me, and I want to thank you for opening up and for trusting me with your dreams and disappointments alike. Please know that you can always depend on me to help in any way, and in the meantime, thank you for being there for me. You are a friend in so many special ways.

Love,
Gail

■ ■ ■

Dear Barbara,

I just wanted to take a moment and thank you for your ability to make me feel so special. Again and again you seem to embrace my thoughts and ideas with such enthusiasm and love, and you listen to my every word. I treasure hearing your ideas, too, as I find you one of the most inspiring and interesting people I know. Thank you for being such a wonderful and special friend.

Love,
Nancy

THANK YOU FOR THINKING OF ME

There are many times in which you appreciate someone simply thinking of you, and you want to acknowledge the person's thoughtfulness. From sad times to happy times, thank you plays a role that expresses your appreciation for someone's thoughts. Here are some notes that say thank you for thinking of me. . . .

Dear Lisa,

There are no words to express my gratitude to you and your wonderful family. I was so comforted to see your faces last week during such a difficult time. Perhaps the only solace in a time of loss is family and close friends. You certainly represented both.

I will always miss my wonderful grandfather, but part of the memories I will cherish are your expressions of caring and kindness during his illness and death.

Love,

Jeryl

■ ■ ■

Dear Christine,

It's hard to find adequate words to thank you for being such a wonderful and thoughtful friend. Thank you for arriving at my door with just the right thing to say. Thank you for being with me when I needed you. You will always remain special to me, and my thanks go to you for being someone I can count on.

Alice

Dear Norma,

Somehow, in your incredibly thoughtful style, you showed up with such a comforting and meaningful gesture. You must have known that anything chocolate would make my day, and your cookies were absolutely delicious. You put a smile on our faces during a trying time. Your friendship continues to make the good times even better, and the difficult times easier to take.

Love,

Phyllis

■ ■ ■

Dear Donna,

Thank you so much for the fabulous bag of magazines while I was recuperating from my recent illness. I always thought I was invincible, but this time I really needed the rest. You knew just the perfect gift. I enjoyed reading all of the magazines; each one helped make staying still and resting much more tolerable. Thank you for thinking of me in such a meaningful way.

Love,

Viki

■ ■ ■

Dear Andy,

Once again, you came to my rescue and I can't thank you enough for thinking of me. You are so busy, and yet you stopped everything to take time out for a visit. It was special to share your wonderful conversation, and I really appreciate the best-seller you selected for me. I promise to share it with you once I finish every word.

Best always,

Austin

Dear Aunt Lois,

Whether I'm well, I'm sick, I'm worried, or absolutely wonderful, you always arrive at my door with your concern and love. You will always be someone I dearly admire and adore, and I just wanted to thank you for thinking of me. It seems my best interest is your top interest, and I feel so fortunate to be your niece. In fact, I relish my position as president of your fan club!

Love always,

Robyn

■ ■ ■

Dear Helen,

During a very difficult and sad time in my life, you came to my rescue. Your kind words, concern, and care served as a great source of strength for me. I will always remember how you supported all of our family in our sorrowful time. Your special deeds will remain close to our hearts.

Thank you for being there for us.

Molly

"Think big thoughts, but relish small pleasures."

— H. JACKSON BROWN, JR.

Edible Thank-Yous

Everyone loves an edible thank-you, especially when it's something that's good to eat, practical, and can be stored or satisfies a craving. Edible thank-yous are abundant, so whenever in doubt . . . give a thank-you that can be eaten up!

When you give an edible thank-you, keep in mind the individual's likes and dislikes. Always find out particular tastes and whether or not the person is able to eat what you send. Sending chocolate to a dieter is deadly! He'll definitely eat it and blame himself later.

Here are some ideas that will be greatly appreciated:

CAKES

Cakes are always a wonderful thank-you, and with all of the different flavors and types, you should be able to match up the perfect cake for the perfect edible thank-you.

You take the cake! Write this little note on a plastic cake knife and wrap up the cake in a box covered with a variety of colored ribbons.

You are the icing on the cake! Any iced cake will do, but here's a way to thank someone who has added a special touch to something that has helped you.

Thank you for making this a piece of cake! This is a wonderful thank-you that tells someone she was helpful and her efforts are appreciated.

You're an absolute angel! Enclose this card with an angel food cake and watch the smiles appear.

OTHER FOOD IDEAS

I would "chews" you again and again as my friend. Fill a basket or bag with bubble gum!

Thank you for using your noodle! Thank someone for his words of wisdom with a basket or bag full of pasta choices. Find gourmet pastas at the grocery and tie ribbons around them. Throw in a jar of sauce and dinner's almost on the table!

Thank you from the bottom of my heart! Low-cholesterol and low-fat foods come in all shapes and sizes. Create a heart-smart thank-you and choose healthy food items that are salt and cholesterol free.

I've gained so much knowing you . . . it's your turn now! Add this card to a basket of serious snack foods, including chocolate, pretzels, candy, cookies—you name it!

To the smartest cookie I know! Bring a friend a basket of cookies or a giant chocolate chip cookie with this message written on it and show your thanks for her words of wisdom.

Thanks for getting me out of a jam! This thank-you would accompany a bag of jams and jellies. It's perfect for someone who helped you get out of a crisis.

Thanks to you, life's a bowl of cherries. Fill a bowl with bing cherries when they are in season.

It's a treat to know you. Fill a basket or bag with candy and lots of delicious treats.

To the sweet smell of your continued success. Send anything edible that's very sweet!

I'd go nuts without you! Send an assortment of nuts or a bag of pistachios.

It's "bean" wonderful knowing you! Thanks a lot. Send a gift of jelly beans to someone you appreciate.

This thanks is for the birds! Give a bag of bird seed with this thank-you to someone who's a bird lover.

My life would be "the pits" without you! Give an assortment of edible items that have pits in them, from cherries to olives to prunes, avocados, and peaches.

*"To have a friend,
be a friend."*

— OLD SAYING

Thank You for the Gift

❧

Many times when you receive a gift, a verbal thank-you is all that is needed. Other times, a more elaborate thank-you does the trick. No matter how you express your thanks, what matters most to those being thanked is knowing that you appreciate the gift and their thoughtfulness is acknowledged.

When you receive a gift in the mail: When someone takes the time to send you a gift by mail, be sure and immediately respond with either a call that you have received it or a thank-you note sent as soon as possible. The giver is often concerned that you didn't get it, so if you can't write a note soon, be sure to relay word somehow that you have received the gift. Be sure also to save the return address on the mailing label. Sometimes that's all you'll have to go by in the event that the enclosure card is misplaced. You'll also have the sender's correct address.

When you receive a gift in person: Opening up a gift in person is easy for some and difficult for others. Comment specifically about the gift, perhaps by saying, "I know just where I will put this vase, and it will be something I always treasure." Try and personalize your response to reflect the gift.

There are two kinds of thank-you notes that people write. There are the ones that carefully reflect someone's innermost feelings and end up being saved, reread over and over; and then there are the one-minute thank-you notes that are written in a hurry and lack that added personal touch.

Some thank-you notes do the job in a few words or less, while others accomplish their goal with lengthy prose. Whatever style thank-you note you write, take a look at some of the following notes and notice what makes them effective. Each note has a few things in common:

HOW TO EXPRESS THANKS FOR A GIFT

- Make your thank-you note specific in its thanks and describe the gift or act of kindness.

- When appropriate, express how you felt when you received it.

- Let the person know that not only her gift is appreciated, but she is, too.

Thank-You Notes

Whether you are a Longfellow at heart, a whiz with words, or someone who stumbles over every sentence with a case of writer's block, you can improve your communication by including the basic ingredients necessary to make your thank-you note effective.

In the meanwhile, here is a collection of thank-you notes that are successful in their presentation and have warmed the hearts of those who received them.

■ ■ ■

Dear Ramona,

Your beautiful gift basket was a feast for my eyes, and truly a gift from the heart. When I opened the door and found it waiting on our doorstep, I was immediately taken by its magnificent presentation.

The fruit basket was too pretty to open, but I was tempted immediately by the delicious display of exotic fruits and divine candies. Your generous gift will always be appreciated, and your unending kindness will always be remembered.

Love always,
Sandy

Dear Phyllis,

How can I ever begin to thank you for the fabulous belt that you gave me for my birthday. Not only will I be right in style, but once again you outdid yourself. Your stylish gift will update my entire wardrobe. How'd you ever know that it was a perfect match with my gold shoes and new purse?

Friends like you make having birthdays such a pleasure.

My warmest thanks always,

Mary

■ ■ ■

Dear Norma,

Whoever said forty was hard to take didn't know my friends! This momentous birthday made me feel like a queen, and I truly adore my new bracelet. The first day I wore it, I received many compliments, and I was proud to say that it's from a very special friend.

Here's to sharing many more happy occasions together, and just remember . . . you're next and I can't wait until it's your turn!

Love,

Betty

Dear Bob,

I can't begin to thank you enough for the fabulous tie that you picked out in honor of my birthday. I was totally taken by surprise, and as you know I have already worn it and am thoroughly enjoying your gift. With all the choices available in ties, I commend you on your ability to select a real winner. Talk about power ties, this one's loaded!

Your good taste prevails. Thank you for your extreme kindness.

Best always,

Alan

■ ■ ■

Dear Lyons,

When your gift arrived I was so surprised, I wish you could have seen my face. The perfume bottle will be a magnificent addition to my collection, and it will always remind me of you. How could I ever thank you for thinking of me in such a personal and thoughtful way?

Love,

Jack

■ ■ ■

Dear Meredith,

I absolutely adored the book you sent me. It reflected such thoughtfulness, and I can't wait to begin reading it. The story must be spectacular if it grabbed your attention, and it will be a welcome break in my busy schedule. Thank you for thinking of me in such a wonderful way. If you don't hear from me for a few days . . . you know I'm glued to your gift!

Thanks again,

Leslie

Dear Lorie,

I simply couldn't resist thanking you for the beautiful picture frame you sent me for my birthday. It looks stunning in our living room. I put a wonderful photograph of my grandparents in it, and together they represent a gift that will always be close to my heart.

I am grateful for our friendship, and I will always remember your thoughtfulness.

Love,

Lisa

■ ■ ■

Dear Mr. and Mrs. Brown,

What a great gift you selected for our new home. You must have heard through the grapevine that we really love antiques. Your beautiful gift will always bring us a great deal of pleasure, and we thank you for adding such a special touch to our new home. We certainly filled it with love; now, thanks to you, we are filling it with beautiful objects of art.

Sincerely,

Laurie and Alan

Dear Aunt Frances,

How can I ever begin to thank you for the gorgeous sweater you chose for my birthday? You are famous in our family for always selecting the perfect gift, and I am lucky indeed to be the recipient. How did you ever know that I needed a white sweater to wear for cool weather? Your sweater will also come in handy when we go on our vacation this year. I plan on proudly wearing it every chance I get.

Thank you again for your continued love and thoughtful ways,

Robyn

■ ■ ■

Dear Cousin Ann,

What a beautiful way to welcome Zachary into the world! The blue and white gingham checked outfit you sent is absolutely adorable, and we can't wait to dress Zachary up for an outing to show him off in it. We feel so blessed now that he has arrived, and we want you to know how much we really appreciated your thoughtful and precious gift. When Zachary grows up, we'll be sure to point out all the photographs in which he wears your outfit and tell him that it was from his very special cousin!

Thanks again.

Love,

Nancy and Steve

Dear Molly,

The flowers you sent me not only brightened my day but added a touch of beauty to our entire home. Every time I walked by the beautiful spring garden bouquet, I thought of your kind gesture and how much you mean to us. While these flowers won't last forever, your lovely gesture will forever remain in our hearts.

Thank you for the meaningful gift.

Love,

Ali

■ ■ ■

Dear Amy,

I absolutely went wild over the piece of hand-blown glass that you sent me for my birthday. You know that I adore objects of art, and this will definitely be one of my prized possessions. Not only will it be constantly admired, but I will always recall your wonderful taste and unending thoughtfulness every time I look at it.

Everything you touch has such a special flair, and how lucky we are to be the recipients of a beautiful gift that has your name all over it.

Love,

Marianne

Dear Alan,

When I received your gift, I was delighted to find such a surprise! The beautiful vase will be a wonderful addition to my art collection, and it will always remind me of your thoughtfulness and excellent taste. Only you, Alan, could have known exactly what I would have picked out myself, and I will always treasure your gift.

Robyn

■ ■ ■

Dear Gloria,

I loved opening my mailbox and finding your delicious chocolate chip cookies. Every one of them melted in my mouth! They were absolutely out of this world, and really hit the spot. Thank you for thinking of me in such a memorable and divine way. I'll get back at you really soon!

Love,
Jaclyn

"Grow old along with me! The best is yet to be, The last of life, for which the first was made."

— ROBERT BROWNING,
RABBI BEN EZRA

Romantic Thank-Yous

R omantic thank-yous are very important, since the ones we care about most often get taken for granted. If this is the case, use these ideas to embrace the one you love and love the one you embrace. Being romantic and showing your appreciation for the one you love takes time and a continuous effort. Ultimately, it can be a wonderful way to add interest and a spark to your relationship.

Showing your thanks will also improve your romantic relationship. Everyone wants to be noticed and appreciated, and the following ideas will give you ways to show your thanks to the one you love.

Romantic thank-yous are most appreciated during the unexpected times. These thank-yous are best when they arrive out of the blue—at times that lift the spirits, show you care, and surprise someone with a thankful thought. Everyone needs to be appreciated, and romantic thank-yous go a long, long way.

> Whoever said friends
> Are an important part of life,
> Must have known you, my love
> Because my best friend's my wife.

Dear Robyn,

I've been thinking about life and love and what you mean to me and this is what I've come up with: Love is a game played by you and me—a walk in the park, a sparkling day at the beach, an adventure shared by you and me. Love is the basis of all actions—of rising and retiring, of striving to fulfill one's ambitions, of facing life as it really is. Love is enjoyment, fulfillment, and growth. Love is disappointment, suspense, and loss and sharing it together. Love is being with you.

Thank you for being my love,

Will

■ ■ ■

Dear Viki,

When you find someone you love, even the simplest moments together are filled with happiness. Thank you for filling my life with your love.

Love,

Paul

■ ■ ■

Dear Annie,

True love is something that never dies; love is always there, never uncertain. Love is not only loving, but being loved. For if you feel that you are being loved, your love becomes even stronger.

Thank you for making my love for you even stronger and for loving me with all your heart,

Morris

Dear Peter,

I want to thank you for always thinking about me when I seem to need you most. While I know you love me, it seems that during those trying times, you are always trying to make me smile and showing your thoughtfulness and love. Thank you for loving me and thank you for being you.

Love,

Jean

TAKE YOUR MATE ON A THANK-YOU DATE

Consider planning a wonderful day, evening, or weekend for your mate or significant other. Here are some great ideas:

Go down memory lane: Plan a day visiting all of your most romantic spots that take you back to special times in your life. Bring along a picnic lunch or your favorite snack and enjoy a visit to the past. Bring along an old photograph book if you have one for some added fun.

Thank-you getaway: Take your significant other on a special getaway. Make all the arrangements, pack his or her bag, and go! Whether it's in town or far away . . . the surprise will be remembered with thanks forever!

More Romantic Thank-Yous

Write I LOVE YOU . . .

in the snow on the back of a car

on the mirror with red lipstick

in ketchup on a hamburger

on a paper heart-shaped doily and put it in his or her briefcase

in icing on a large cookie or cake!

Send flowers to work and a note that says, *"Love, Your secret admirer."*

Give your mate an excess amount of his or her favorite candy . . .

Red licorice tied in knots: *"I'm glad we tied the knot!"*

Hundreds of chocolate kisses: *"Your kisses are sweeter than these!"*

Hide "I Love You" notes in the refrigerator on your partner's favorite foods.

Thank You, Mom . . .
Thank You, Dad . . .
Thank You, Family

TO MY MOTHER,
THERE COULD BE NO OTHER

Being a mother is joyous and needs no thank-yous; however, they sure feel wonderful when they are given. So think of ways you can thank Mom all year long. If you are a mom, be sure to save your children's thank-yous. They become beautiful mementoes later in life and serve as a reminder of your love for each other.

■ ■ ■

Dear Mom,

How can I ever begin to thank you for doing what you love so much . . . being my mom. You have taught me so much about life and continue to serve as my inspiration daily. Your thoughts, ideas, and advice continue to guide all of my decisions and the way in which I approach everything. I am so fortunate and blessed that you are my mother.

I will love you always,

Robyn

Dedicated to My Mother

When I was young, not foolish but not wise, I knew that I had a hero who would help me through my troubles, although she was faceless. Now I have gotten wise and she is no longer faceless.

Kimberly Coburn, age 7

■ ■ ■

Dear Mom,

If I tried to count every time you've gone out of your way or done something to help me, I'd be counting in the millions. Your unending devotion to my happiness and well-being will always be appreciated. I wish I could find the words to thank you for your unconditional love. You are truly an inspiration in my life, and knowing how much you love me serves as my daily motivation.

With love and thanks always,

Ava

■ ■ ■

Dear Mom,

You said I was great and I believed you, and I went on to do great things. You then said I was kind and I believed you, and I went on to do kind deeds. You then said I was loved and I believed you, and I went on to do loving and thoughtful things. Thanks to you, I am who you have helped me to be and I have you to thank.

My love and thanks always,

Ali

THANK YOU, DAD

When I was a little girl, I called my father the Marshmallow Daddy. That's because he was such a softie and I was the apple of his eye. Today on his desk at his office sits a clay dog that I made for him when I was a little girl, and he saved all of my greeting cards and poems that I wrote over the years. He truly taught me acts of kindness, and that showing kindness and compassion for others is one of the most important traits you can have.

Thank you, Dad! Three special words that mean I love you. There are many ways to thank your dad for being there, for loving you, and for guiding you. The following ideas might spark some ways that you can say thanks to your dad.

■ ■ ■

Dear Dad,

Thanks to all your encouragement, I grew up believing I could do anything I set my mind to. I will always remember and appreciate the little things you've done for me. I can now assure you that they've added up to very big things. You have given me self-confidence, the ability to appreciate others for who they are, and a streamline of unstoppable determination and optimism. The values you have taught me will always reinforce what really matters in life. And when it comes to what matters, you'll always be at the top of the list.

I love you,
Robyn

Dear Dad,

Sometimes I forget to stop and thank you for being such a terrific dad, but I hope this note of appreciation will let you know.
You have served as my guiding force in everything I do. I have
always treasured your approval, and you have always given it no
matter what. You gave me the room to grow into who I am today,
and the values and judgment to know what's right. I will be eternally indebted to you, and feel so fortunate that you are my
father. You are a remarkable example of a truly perfect dad! I'm
so lucky you're mine.

Love,

Justin

THANK-YOUS TO OTHER
MEMBERS OF YOUR FAMILY

Some of the most important relationships right within your
reach are with your family. So often we get caught up in our
daily activities and forget to stop and think of those who are
closest to us. One of life's greatest treasures is to know your rel-
atives and take the time to cherish these relationships.

The Family Tree

Your entire family will thank you if you create a family tree for
everyone. What a wonderful thank-you gift to preserve and
treasure over the years. Your homemade family tree should list
everyone's birth dates, and a poem written to go with it would
be especially nice.

Dear Doug,

While I'm sure that I've grown up taking you for granted, I just wanted you to know that one of the greatest things in my life has been having you as my brother. I might act like your opinion doesn't matter, but I want you to know that I have listened to your every word. Over the years it's been your advice and concern for my well-being that has helped me in so many ways. I am eternally grateful for your big-brother advice, and for your love and wishes for my happiness.

I might not say it often, but I do love you.

Love,
Robyn

■ ■ ■

Dear Deana,

A kid sister is far from what I ever thought I'd need in life, but you changed that thought. You came along and disturbed my room, most of my belongings, and many of my private telephone calls. Growing up with you was truly a pain. But all of those little problems are now remembered with great affection, for I really loved having a little sister who thought I was the greatest big sister on earth. I might not have given you a lot of attention, but you will always be my little sister, and I will always love you in a great big way.

Love,
Lala

Dear Aunt Hariette,

I count my blessings often because I realize how very fortunate I am to have such a wonderful aunt like you. You have served as such an inspiration for me, and I have tried to pattern much of my life after your kind and loving ways. I am always so proud to tell people you are my relative and my friend as well. In your case the name aunt stands for Absolutely Unbelievable Nice and Terrific! That's my Aunt Hariette!

Love,

Linda

■ ■ ■

Dear Grandma and Grandpa,

As you have loved and love your children, you have passed on to their children the greatest gift of all, the gift of grandparenting. You have served such an important role in my life, and I hope you know how much you mean to me. Growing up as the apple of your eye made me feel that no matter what I did you'd always be there to support me. Your praise and affection have been unconditional, and I forever thank you for your unending affection. You will remain in my heart always with the deepest of love and admiration.

Love,

Justin

Dear Justin,

Having you for a child has been, without question, the greatest pleasure in my entire life. Since you were very little, I have marveled at your every step and accomplishment. I know that sometimes you and I don't see eye to eye, but always know that you have been my greatest teacher in life. Your opinion and feelings will always matter to me, and my greatest wish for you is that you find happiness and purpose throughout your entire life.

I will forever be your greatest fan, and want you to know I am here for you always.

I love you always,
Mom

■ ■ ■

Dear Cindy,

Just a few words to say it was such a joy to be with you yesterday for a few hours, as we watched Mandy play softball for Galloway. Thanks for inviting me to join you. The best gift of all for any grandparent is to have the opportunity to share in the fun and good times of children and grandchildren. My family is my top priority in life and I love each of you very much.

Stay happy, stay healthy.

Love,
Dad

"One can never pay in gratitude; one can only pay 'in kind' somewhere else in life."

— ANNE MORROW LINDBERGH

Thank You for Dinner

~✺~

Whenever you go to someone's home for dinner, you have a wonderful opportunity to show your thanks in a special way. It's nice to bring along a thank-you gift, and a thank-you note later always has meaning.

Great thank-you for dinner gifts include:

Arrive with a basket of colorful napkins with a saying on them that fits your host!

Bring a dozen fresh bagels with cream cheese and jellies for the next morning.

Send fresh flowers the day of the dinner with a special card.

If your hosts collect something, bring a book about their collection or another item to enhance it.

Bring anything monogrammed with their initials or name.

If they have children, bring a surprise for the kids.

Bring a copy of *The Thank-You Book* for the ultimate thanks!

Here are some ideas to help you say thank you for dinner:

Your dinner was so divine,
I'm glad that you're a friend of mine.

You treated me just like a king.
Thank you, friend, for everything!

I'll never get thinner . . .
If you're cooking dinner.

Thank you for a wonderful time,
Your dinner was so divine.

THANK-YOU NOTES

Dear Ava and Bob,

Dinner was absolutely wonderful; we enjoyed every single bite! You must have spent hours preparing each of those gourmet recipes, and we can't thank you enough for your generous hospitality and unwavering friendship. Great friends and great food . . . what a combination! You both are so wonderful—we really love you!

Thanks again for a memorable evening.

Robyn and Willy

Dear Aunt Ramona,

We all felt like royalty at your beautiful dinner last Saturday night. Fit for a king and queen, every course of your delicious menu will always be savored and remembered. I don't recall ever seeing such a gorgeous table setting in my entire life—leave it to you to have thought of every detail!

Our sincerest thanks for such a wonderful evening. We're slowly coming back down to earth!

Best always,

Leslie

■ ■ ■

Dear Mary,

I don't know when we have ever enjoyed such a fabulous evening. The food was divine and the company sensational. Your culinary talents never cease to amaze us as you always discover the most outrageous recipes. I'm still thinking about your sweet potato soufflé. We're all waiting for you to write a cookbook . . . we'll be first in line to buy it!

Our warmest thanks again,

Freeda

"The most exquisite pleasure is giving pleasure to others."

— JEAN DE LA BRUYÈRE

Thank You, Teacher

In everyone's life are teachers who really make a difference, and as we grow older we recall how they believed in us along the way. Teachers deserve a great big thank-you daily, and here are some ways that you or your children can thank the teachers you know.

Dear Mr. Pepe,

I can't begin to tell you how much you meant to me as a teacher. You served as an individual who expected the very best from all of us, and taught us how to deliver it. Besides that, you made achieving and believing in ourselves an exciting opportunity. Thank you for your patience and enthusiasm. You really made learning a fun adventure.

Sincerely,
Robyn

■ ■ ■

Dear Mrs. Harris,

When I first met you, I saw the kind of person I was proud to call my teacher. Every day when you came to school, you had a smile on your face and a kind word for all of your students. Your love of learning ignited our curiosity and made learning so much fun. You taught us all to appreciate neatness and how to pay attention to details. You will never know how much your guidance has helped me, but I wanted you to know that you have made a big difference in my life.

My thanks always,

Phil

Feature your teacher: Use this idea to feature your teacher on the cover of a well-known magazine. For example, cut out the face of the teacher you want to thank and glue her face on the cover of one of the leading tabloids or beauty magazines. You could computerize or write your own caption . . . WORLD'S GREATEST TEACHER AWARDED!

Write now! Write a story about what your teacher has meant to you and send it to her. For example, fill in the blanks . . .

Dear Mrs. Gill,

I just wanted to take a minute to thank you for being such a wonderful teacher. In your class I learned _____.

You are very special because _____ _____.
I will always remember _____.

One day I know I'll look back and remember _____.

You will always have a special fan . . . that's me!

Sincerely,

David

Make a list: Think of all the things your teacher has taught you during the year, and when you write him a note, make a book or a scroll-style letter that lists them: FIFTY THINGS MR. MILMAN TAUGHT ME

■ ■ ■

As teachers go
You are the best.
You shine above
All the rest.
So accept my thanks
For all you do
I'm very lucky
Because my teacher's you.

How can I thank you?
Let me count the ways.
Thank you for 200
very special days!

An apple for our teacher
Would never be enough,
For teaching us about the world
And lots of other stuff.
But perhaps a world of thank-yous is what we all should say,
To tell you, teacher, how much you mean to all of us each day.
So thank you, our dear teacher, for everything you do,
We all feel very lucky
That each of us has you!

"Nothing great was ever achieved without enthusiasm."

— RALPH WALDO EMERSON,
CIRCLES

Business Thank-Yous

The people with whom and for whom you work will appreciate your thank-yous. Here are some ideas that are great for your employees, boss, friends, co-volunteers, or anyone at your workplace.

THANK YOU, VOLUNTEER

Without your volunteering
We wouldn't be the same . . .
You really made a difference
And helped us rise to fame.

THANK YOU, BOSS

Every boss is different, and your thank-you must match the protocol that you feel your boss will appreciate. Some bosses are conservative and will appreciate a card or note, while others love constant reminders of your appreciation. You make the decision as to what would be appropriate and then consider some of these suggestions.

One clever way to thank a boss is to find out exactly what he is interested in. If your boss loves to fish, bring him some fishing magazines—and tell him everything will be under control when he goes fishing!

Give your boss a trophy that is engraved . . .

WORLD'S BEST BOSS.

Thank you for the suggestion! Consider thanking your boss when she gives you constructive criticism. Let her know what you learned from it and you will come out like a winner.

Robyn, Robyn, Robyn,

What can we say, where do we begin? Claudia and I are very proud of the friendship that has developed between you and our family. If you treat other "clients" the same as us, your roster of friends must be a mile long. Your guidance has been incredible . . . you're special to us!

Thanks for the books, the articles, everything,

Pat, Claudia, Lindsey, and Hunter

■ ■ ■

Dear Cindy,

Working with you is such a pleasure. In fact, whenever we are meeting, it doesn't feel like work at all. You have taught me so much about being a professional, and I will always value your advice. Thank you for being a wonderful role model.

Sincerely,

Ruth

THANK-YOUS FOR CO-WORKERS

Lollipop thank-you: Bring a basket of lollipops to the office with a note that says, "Thanks for helping me lick the problem!"

Bubble gum basket: Bring a basket of bubble gum with a note that says, "Thank you for your help . . . without you I would have blown it!"

A piece of cake: Bring a cake for the office and include a note, "Working with you is a piece of cake!"

Secretary Day: Make every day Secretary Day and leave the secretary notes of appreciation!

"The heart that loves is always young."

— ANONYMOUS
(GREEK PROVERB)

Kid-Sized Thanks

Here's help for the kids you know who either need to write a lot of thank-you notes or need assistance for the occasional one that pops up. When our children were little, we always had a thank-you rule: "You thank someone first before enjoying their gift." And what an incentive that was . . . after a big thank-you to Grandma, which of course earned a big smile, the reward was the opportunity to have fun! More importantly, everyone ended up feeling good and Grandma knew she was appreciated.

In addition to the thank-you rule, over the years whenever I received a thank-you note, I would read it to our kids and let them tell me what they thought about it. From the content of the note, I would ask if they could describe to me what I gave the person? Did the writer sound appreciative? Did he or she like my gift? And last but not least, was the note personally written just for me, or could it have been written to 100 other people, too?

Over the years, Justin and Ali learned how to write meaningful thank-yous that conveyed their feelings and consequently, their notes received rave reviews. The best by-product of all was that our children learned how good saying "thank you" really does feel and that a thank-you is a meaningful gift when sent from the heart.

When children start expressing their thanks at a young age, it becomes a way of life. So get the kids started early with a thank-you call, their own personalized stationery, or art materials for that special crayon drawing. Children will experience firsthand how wonderful it feels to say thank you! Our son Justin, who is in college, and our daughter Ali continue to make a point of expressing their appreciation, no matter how big or small a gesture. In fact, fourteen-year-old Ali is the author of *The Thank You Book for Kids*, which illustrates hundreds of thank-you notes, tips, and good deeds you can do every day. I'm grateful to have her assistance in spreading my thank-you mission.

Since kids really do say the smartest things, I went straight to the source and asked children I know to help me with notes that they'd write. Here are some of their examples to help you get started.

■ ■ ■

Dear Aunt Janet,

Thank you so much for the globe you gave me for my birthday. It has both a special place in my room and my heart. It means so much to me to see how you went out of your way to find a gift so fitting. I cannot tell you how excited I was when I opened it. The loving card you attached almost meant more to me than the globe itself.

Love,
Jared

Dear Mr. and Mrs. Freedman,

I would like to thank you for remembering me in such a generous way on my Bar Mitzvah. Although I don't know how I will spend the money, I promise I will put it to good use.

Thanks again,

Bart C.

■ ■ ■

Dear Nana and Poppy,

How could I have asked for a better gift? It was as if you read my mind to discover that all I wanted was a puppy. He is the most adorable thing I have ever seen in my life. His ears point up when I call him. I will always love this puppy, and every time I look at him I am reminded of you. This birthday will surely be one I will never forget. Come over soon and see all the new tricks I have taught him. You will be amazed.

Love always,

David

■ ■ ■

Dear Grandma and Grandpa,

Awesome! That's the perfect word to describe the sweater you gave me. I know you think I don't always like to dress up, but with your neat sweater, I now have an incentive. I like all the colors in it and will wear it next time I need to look great.

Thanks again,

Pete

Dear Frank,

Thank you so much for the beautiful butterfly pin. It's gorgeous! I've gotten so many compliments on it. The electric blue matches my eyes very nicely. The pin was definitely one of my favorite gifts.

Sincerely,
Lauren McKinney

■ ■ ■

Dear Mom and Dad,

Thanks so much for the wonderful birthday gift. A CD player is the perfect gift for a 13-year-old. I'm positive that I will be using it a lot. Maybe if you're lucky I'll let you use it. Well, anyway, I couldn't have asked for a better and more usable gift. Thanks again! Love ya always.

Your daughter,
Mandy Rollins

■ ■ ■

Dear Lynn,

Thank you very much for showing my artwork in your gallery. It has given me the support I need to continue working on my art. I never thought that I would be showing artwork at age 12. You have certainly changed my life considerably. Thank you once again.

Sincerely,
Baleigh Isaacs

Dear Mom and Dad,

Thank you so much for making the 12 years of my life as great as they are. I appreciate you taking me everywhere I want and need to go. I know sometimes you can't keep up with me, but you try. Thank you again.

Your son,

Justin

■ ■ ■

Dear Mrs. Spizman,

Thank you so much for putting together this book. I really enjoy writing, and I am fairly good at it. Your book is my first real chance to have one of my writings published in anything besides the school literary magazine, which I truly enjoy taking part in. I know that the chance of you picking my writing for your book is very slim, but I hope that you will at least consider it. Thank you so much for reading my letter, and I hope you have a great day.

Yours truly,

Matt Lerner

■ ■ ■

Dear Mrs. Spizman,

Thank you for taking the Dearman/Daugherty class to see you on TV last year. I always wanted to see actual people being filmed while on TV. Now that I've had the chance I'm even more interested than I was before. I thought it was a really nice gesture, considering how noisy the guys can be. Thanks again!

Sincerely,

Mikalee Greeson

Dear Tom,

Thank you for that fishing trip. Life is a lot better now that I really know how to fish. My future is a lot brighter because now when people ask me, "Do you want to go fishing?" I can say, "Yes," and I won't have to ask them for help. I can simply go with them and go off on my own and catch some fish and walk back to the group and watch them with their mouths hanging open wondering how I caught all those fish. Thanks, again, for teaching me a skill I will use all my life.

Sincerely,

Joseph Lawsky

■ ■ ■

Dear Gamy,

Thank you for the skirt you made me, and for helping me finish my dollhouse. The skirt is beautiful and I have gotten many compliments on it. Don't worry, I will be over there again soon to work on my dollhouse. Thank you, again, and don't forget that you'll always be my favorite Grandma.

Sincerely,

Alenna Smith

■ ■ ■

Dear Grandma,

Thanks for the twenty dollars you gave me. I know you never know what to get me. I'm very sure I will use it to buy something I want. I also enjoyed the card you gave me. Thank you very much.

Sincerely,

Rob Stevens

Dear Tim,

Thank you so much for being a great friend. You have helped me through bad times and good, and you always make me feel better. When I call or write, you always give me a boost of self-confidence. You make me feel better when I'm sad and you always cheer me up when I'm down in the dumps.

I love you,
Rachel Lovell

■ ■ ■

Dear Michael and Orah,

Thank you so much for coming to my Bar Mitzvah. I love the poem book. When I saw it I couldn't believe that it was from 1929. I liked the way that the pictures of the writers were next to every poem. It was the most generous gift that you could have given me.

Sincerely,
Brielle Gould
P.S. I hope Orah had fun!

■ ■ ■

Dear Grandpa,

Hi, how are you doing? I hope you're doing fine! I got the CD player that you sent me for my birthday. Thank you so much. It is the very best present I've had this year. It's great! I listen to it all the time. I went to the mall and got some new CD's with my mom and my brother. It is the best. Thank you.

Love,
Farhana Sulten

Dear Great-Aunt Thelma,

I hope your Thanksgiving was as nice as mine. I just adored the pasta maker you sent me. For Thanksgiving we ate almost nothing but pasta from it. Thank you very much for the jumper. The matching beret is lovely. How is Uncle Horace doing since the heart attack? I hope he is out of the hospital. Please write back. Thanks again!

Love,

Your great-niece,

Vanessa Zboreak

■ ■ ■

Dear Grandpa,

Thank you for coming to visit on Thanksgiving. I really enjoyed our walks to the park and all the interesting talks we had. I wish you didn't live so far away in Maine, but I guess that just makes our visits more special. How's Grandma? I'm sure she's fine. Have you been swimming or jogging lately? I started the swim team and I'm meeting more people and making new friends. I'm also having a lot of fun, even though I have to wake up at 7:15 in the morning. I've got to go to swim-team practice now. Thanks, again, for coming.

Love always,

Addie Johnson

P.S. Please write back.

Dear Aunt Martine,

Thank you for the cactus you gave me for my birthday. You didn't tell me it was a flowering one. I came home one day and it had a beautiful yellow blossom. It blooms about twice a month. It's the perfect plant for me because it's very easy to take care of. Thank you for remembering my birthday.

Your loving niece,

Jessica Gould

P.S. What is the cactus called?

■ ■ ■

Dear Grandma and Alex,

Thank you for the great baseball computer game. It's extremely interesting how you use old-time baseball players like Babe Ruth, Hank Aaron, and Lou Gehrig. I love the closeups and all the exciting plays. I play it every day. So far it is the most exciting game I have. The graphics are amazing.

How are you guys? Have you been doing well? Are you doing well playing golf? We're in the middle of autumn here, and the leaves on the trees are beautiful. Are there any trees down there that have changed color? Well, I miss you. Come visit me sometime soon.

Love,

Evan Steiner

Dear Mr. Long,

Thank you so much for coming and speaking about the Ogalala Indians. Our school was very lucky to have you here. After you spoke, I realized that everyone is the same, but we all have different clothes, customs, and cultures. Thanks, again, for taking the time to come and speak.

Sincerely,

Rachel Fox

■ ■ ■

Dear Francisca,

I loved going to your wedding. It was a lot of fun. I especially liked being the flower girl. It was so sweet of you to give me flower-girl paper dolls. I play with them all the time. My sister Rebekah loved being the bridesmaid. She told me to tell you she loved your wedding dress. I am going to be seven years old soon. Since I caught the flower bouquet, maybe I'll have a wedding instead of a birthday party. Just kidding!

Sincerely,

Your favorite cousin,

Rachel Barry

■ ■ ■

Dear Mr. and Mrs. H. Jackson Brown,

Thank you so much for the fabulous pen. In fact, I'm writing this with it right now. I hope maybe one day I can have the writing skills and be as famous as you. I think you are a great writer.

From a writer to a writer, this is a perfect gift.

Justin Spizman

Dear Aunt Libby,

I love the sweater, earrings, and rings you gave me. I think I will wear them in the school play. Also, the silver ring you gave me for my birthday is really nice. Everyone likes it. I let my best friend borrow the sweater and she loves it, too. Thank you so much, and something is coming to you in the mail because you are the greatest.

Sincerely,

Sarah Zeeman

■ ■ ■

Dear Grandma and Grandpa,

Thank you for visiting me on my mother's funeral. I think it helped me to spend time with you. I can't wait to see you.

Sincerely,

Evan Grodin

■ ■ ■

Dear Cousins,

When I opened your gift, I had the biggest smile on my face. I couldn't believe my eyes when I saw the gorgeous necklace. Thank you for thinking of me in such a generous way. I will treasure it forever and remember the love that came with it every time I wear it. Whenever I get a compliment, I'll be sure to give you all the credit for having such beautiful taste. You mean the world to me and I appreciate your thoughtfulness more than you'll ever know.

With endless hugs and smiles,

Ali

"A joy that's shared is a joy made double."

— ANONYMOUS,
recorded by John Ray,
English Proverbs

Homemade and Recycled Thanks

A nything homemade has a special meaning because it shows that you took the time to add your special touch.

Homemade Chocolate Chip Cookies. This thank-you will disappear very quickly! Add a note to a tin of freshly baked chocolate chip cookies that says, "To one of the smartest cookies we know, our thanks always."

Hot Chocolate. Mix a store-bought brand of powdered hot chocolate with a little cinnamon and add your own label that says, "Our warmest thanks."

Souper Soups. Soups are always a winner when it's cold outside, so take a portion to a friend next time you cook up a great soup and attach a note that says, "To a souper friend."

Address Book. Make a friend an address book filled with VIP friends' and family's addresses. Add special dates and this will be a gift that's really appreciated! Attach a card that says, "I will always have your number, hope you enjoy having these!"

Super Snack Trail Mix. Mix up peanuts, healthy cereal pieces, miniature pretzels, mini-marshmallows, M&M's, or anything your heart desires, and create a jar filled with this super snack. Include a card that reads, "Thanks a munch."

Rainbow Jar. Layer colorful candy, nuts, or anything that will not melt in a jar to create a rainbow effect. I like to recycle a coffee jar: clean it out, remove the label, and let it dry thoroughly. Then I begin adding colorful candy one layer at a time, creating an adorable gift that will be eaten up. Include a card that says, "Hope this brightens your day."

No Bologna—Just a Great Big Thanks. With a little imagination, you can transform a good deed into a clever gift that will bring a smile to anyone's face. Bring a deli platter to a friend's door for a fun thank-you. Or assemble a lox and bagel platter and add a note that reads, "Thanks a lox."

Basket Case. Assemble a basket filled with delicious goodies to thank a friend or family member for being there when you need them most. Include a note that says, "I'd be a basket case without you. Thanks for coming to my rescue!"

An Irresistible Thank-You. There are so many treats and sweets that can't be resisted. Fill a colorful tote bag with items you adore and deliver them with a card that says, "We couldn't resist saying thanks. Hope you can't resist these, either!"

A Corny Thank-You. Popcorn is a favorite among all ages, so give or send a tin filled with popcorn or a basket jam-packed with microwave or stove-top popcorns. Include clever sayings such as "Thanks to the world's best Pop!" or "I'm popping with thank-yous" or even "Hope you'll pop in soon and come see us!"

A Wonderful Pair. Here's a delicious way to thank a friend or family member who paired up with you recently and was helpful. Fill a basket with pears and thank a friend or pair of friends for being so special. Or, personalize a bag of apples with "You're the apple of my eye!"

Truffles to the Rescue. Truffles are always a divine way to cheer someone up. Choose your favorite truffles and add a note that says, "Take one of these a day and enjoy it . . . with thanks from me!"

Lots of Labels. Personalized address labels are time-savers and a gift that will be greatly appreciated. They are easy to create on your computer. Purchase self-sticking pages of labels and print a collection of return address and mailing labels in an appealing selection of fonts and styles. Also include gift labels that are perfect for saying thank-you, such as "A World of Thanks. Love, the Spizmans."

Shower with Thanks. If you ever want to shower someone with thanks, fill a basket with shower gels and body lotions for some well-deserved rest and relaxation. Add some soothing soaps and bath beads for a totally indulgent gift that will really be enjoyed.

A Garden of Thanks. When the seasons change, it's often a perfect time to plant flowers or bulbs for a special family member or friend. I'll never forget the time my cousin Scott surprised us and replanted the planters at our front door with a beautiful array of mixed flowers. It was a hectic period for us and I didn't have time. He brightened the entry to our home with his special talent and gave us a gift of the season that I'll lovingly remember.

Thanks to a Tea! Fill a mug with flavored teas and wrap it up in colorful cellophane for a special friend who warms your heart. Add a ribbon and you have an instant gift that will make someone's day.

RECYCLED THANKS

"Thank you" comes in all shapes and sizes, and some really clever ideas are right at your fingertips waiting to be recycled. Think of all the items that you might throw out daily, and challenge yourself to recycle them. Here are some ideas:

Can Do. Clean out tin cans of any shape or size and cover any sharp spots around the rim with tape, if necessary. Cover the can with remnants of wrapping paper or wallpaper scraps and trim off any excess. Tape or glue the covering in place. To finish off the can, tie a ribbon in a bow around it. This will make a wonderful planter or pencil holder. Fill the can with the object of your choice.

Clever Coasters. Save the plastic lids from a variety of containers and stack them in a pile. Tie a ribbon around them and give them as clever coasters. They really come in handy when you need them.

THANK-YOU GIFT WRAPS

You can make your thank-you memorable with a special gift wrap. Here are some of my favorites.

Box in a Box. Wrap your small gift in a small box and then wrap the wrapped-up gift in a larger box. The search for the gift is half the fun!

Recycle It! Save your cereal boxes, containers, and colorful bags that candy comes in, and use them for a clever gift wrap.

Give a Gift in a Gift. One of my favorite ways to give a thank-you gift is in a gift itself. Search for beautiful silk boxes or a pretty child's container and put your thank-you gift in one of these. The container remains a lovely reminder long after you give the gift.

A Jewel of a Gift Wrap. When giving jewelry, create a memorable delivery by putting a necklace on a beautiful doll for a young child or carefully piercing the ears on a soft stuffed animal with a pair of earrings. Or, wrap the jewelry in a beautiful box, then sit the box in the arms of a child's favorite stuffed animal. Place it by her bedside to surprise her when she wakes up in the morning.

OTHER BOOKS THAT SAY THANK YOU

There are many thoughtful books out there about giving thanks and gratitude, and any one of them would make a fine thank-you gift for a family member or friend. Here are my favorites.

The Thank You Book for Kids: Hundreds of Creative, Cool, and Clever Ways to Say Thank You! Ali Lauren Spizman, Longstreet Press, 2001. Thank-you words to add: *"I thank my lucky stars for a kid like you!"*

The Perfect Present: The Ultimate Gift Guide for Every Occasion. Robyn Freedman Spizman, Crown Publishers, 1999. Thank-you words to add: *"It's friends (or family) like you who matter most."*

Chicken Soup for the Soul: 101 Stories to Open the Heart and Rekindle the Spirit. Jack Canfield and Mark Victor Hansen, Health Communications, 1993. Thank-you words to add: *"You're my chicken soup for the soul."*

Life's Little Instruction Book. H. Jackson Brown, Jr., Rutledge Hill Press, 1988. Thank-you words to add: *"I'd follow your instructions anywhere!"*

The New International Dictionary of Quotations. Selected by Hugh Rawson & Margaret Miner, Signet, 1988. Thank-you words to add: *"Quote me on this . . . you deserve a world of thanks."*

A Gift from the Sea. Anne Morrow Lindbergh, Pantheon Books, 1991. Thank-you words to add: *"With an ocean of thanks!"*

From Me to You. JacLynn Morris & Paul L. Fair, Ph.D., Writer's Digest Books, 2000. Thank-you words to add: *"With thanks forever from me to you."*

Random Acts of Kindness. Editors of Conairi Press, 1993. Thank-you words to add: *"Thank you for your endless acts of kindness."*

PEOPLE I WISH TO THANK

Scott Bard, Barbara Babbit Kaufman, Robyn Richardson, Tysie Whitman, Jill Dible, Amy Burton, Ruth Waters, Thomas Cogburn, and all the fabulous people at Longstreet Press. Thanks also go to Chuck Perry, Suzanne Comer Bell, Pauline Blonder, Francis Ritchkin, Saul Becker, Bert Paisley, Jared Heyman, Patty Brown, Bart Cohen, Pat and Claudia Simpson, Janice Hughes, principal of middle learning, and students at the Galloway School, Dr. Marianne Garber, H. Jackson Brown, Jr., and Rosemary Brown, Joe Aronoff, Cindy Dearman, Ava Wilensky, Bob Brechko, Lorie Lewis, Chris Rambo, Mary Lynn Ryan, Laurie Selzer, Betty Sunshine, Carla Lovell, Donna Weinstock, Norma Gordon, Nancy Freedman, Gail Heyman, Bettye Storne, and Jack Morton.

OTHER BOOKS BY ROBYN SPIZMAN

The Perfect Present: The Ultimate Gift Guide for Every Occasion

When Words Matter Most: Thoughtful Words and Deeds to Express Just the Right Thing at Just the Right Time

Bet You Didn't Know: Smart Answers for Every Aspect of Your Life

Kids on Board: Fun Things to Do While Commuting or Road Tripping with Children

300 Incredible Things to Learn on the Internet (with Ken Leebow)

300 Incredible Things for Women on the Internet (with Ken Leebow)

The Super Shopper Series: Quick Tips for Busy People

Life's Little Instruction Book for Incurable Romantics (with H. Jackson Brown, Jr.)

A Hero in Every Heart (with H. Jackson Brown, Jr.)

Monsters under the Bed (with Drs. Stephen and Marianne Garber)

Good Behavior (with Drs. Stephen and Marianne Garber)

Lollipop Grapes & Clothespin Critters: Remedies for Restless Children